UNITED ARAB EMIRATES 2016 HUMAN RIGHTS REPORT

EXECUTIVE SUMMARY

The United Arab Emirates (UAE) is a federation of seven semiautonomous emirates with a resident population of approximately 9.2 million, of whom an estimated 11 percent are citizens. The rulers of the seven emirates constitute the Federal Supreme Council, the country's highest legislative and executive body. The council selects a president and a vice president from its membership, and the president appoints the prime minister and cabinet. Sheikh Khalifa bin Zayed Al Nahyan, ruler of Abu Dhabi emirate, is president, although Crown Prince Mohammed bin Zayed Al Nahyan of Abu Dhabi exercises most executive authority. The emirates are under patriarchal rule with political allegiance defined by loyalty to tribal leaders, leaders of the individual emirates, and leaders of the federation. A limited, appointed electorate participates in periodic elections for the partially elected Federal National Council (FNC), a consultative body that examines, reviews, and recommends changes to legislation and may discuss topics for legislation. The FNC consists of 40 representatives allocated proportionally to each emirate based on population; half are elected members while the remainder are appointed by the leaders of their respective emirates. There are no political parties. The last election was in October 2015, when an appointed electorate of approximately 224,000 citizens, making up one-fifth of the total citizen population, elected 20 FNC members. Citizens may express their concerns directly to their leaders through traditional consultative mechanisms such as the open majlis (forum).

Civilian authorities maintained effective control over the security forces.

The three most significant human rights problems were the inability of citizens to choose their government in free and fair periodic elections; limitations on civil liberties (including the freedoms of speech, press, assembly, and association); and arrests without charge, incommunicado detentions, lengthy pretrial detentions, and mistreatment during detention.

Other reported human rights problems included a lack of government transparency; police and prison guard brutality; government interference with privacy rights, including arrests and detentions for internet postings or commentary; and a lack of judicial independence. The law directly prohibits blasphemy and proselytizing by non-Muslims, and indirectly prohibits conversion from Islam by referring to Sharia law on matters of religious doctrine. Domestic abuse and violence against women

remained problems. Noncitizens faced legal and societal discrimination. Legal and societal discrimination against persons with HIV/AIDS and based on sexual orientation and gender identity remained problems. Trafficking in persons, mistreatment including physical and sexual abuse of foreign domestic servants and other migrant workers, and discrimination against persons with disabilities remained problems. The government restricted worker rights. Lack of transparency and access made it difficult to assess the extent of many reported human rights problems, such as conditions surrounding detentions in state security cases, social and legal discrimination, and societal abuses of women and children.

The government investigated, prosecuted, and brought to conviction cases of official corruption. There were no reports of impunity involving security forces during the year.

Section 1. Respect for the Integrity of the Person, Including Freedom from:

a. Arbitrary Deprivation of Life and other Unlawful or Politically Motivated Killings

There were no reports the government or its agents committed arbitrary or unlawful killings.

b. Disappearance

There were reports of disappearances of individuals allegedly involved in state security cases. For example, according to human rights organizations, Emirati citizen Abdulrahman Bin Sobeih disappeared in December 2015 after authorities in Indonesia arrested him and handed him over to UAE authorities. The status of Bin Sobeih, who had previously been convicted in absentia for membership in a group affiliated with the Muslim Brotherhood, was unknown until he appeared before the National Security Court of the Federal Supreme Court in March. Nongovernmental organizations (NGOs) reported that on November 14, Bin Sobeih was sentenced to 10 years in prison and three years of administrative control subsequent to the completion of his sentence for belonging to a secret organization. Additionally, several persons were arrested in 2015 and their whereabouts were unknown until the following year. Examples include Nassir bin Ghaith and Tayseer al-Najjar (see sections 1.d. and 2.a. respectively).

c. Torture and Other Cruel, Inhuman, or Degrading Treatment or Punishment

The constitution prohibits such practices, and there were no reports of instances. There were reports in previous years that some individuals imprisoned for suspected state security violations were subjected to severe abuse or mistreatment. Human rights groups alleged this mistreatment took place during interrogations and to induce a prisoner to sign a confession. For example, in 2015 Human Rights Watch (HRW) reported allegations from prisoners that authorities used techniques including beatings, forced standing, and threats to rape or kill, including by electrocution. Two Libyan-Americans arrested on security-related grounds in August 2014 said they were tortured while in detention. In some cases, judges ordered investigations, to include medical examinations by state-appointed doctors, into allegations of torture or mistreatment. The government-sanctioned Emirates Human Rights Association, which monitors prisons, reported in December that it had not found any human rights violations related to treatment of detainees during the year.

Sharia (Islamic law) courts, which adjudicate criminal and family law cases, may impose flogging as punishment for adultery, prostitution, consensual premarital sex, pregnancy outside marriage, defamation of character, and drug or alcohol abuse, although this was rare and tended to be confined to only a few jurisdictions. Multiple Western consulates reported courts imposed flogging as a punishment in some of the northern emirates.

Prison and Detention Center Conditions

Prison conditions varied widely among the individual emirates and between regular prisons and state security detention facilities.

<u>Physical Conditions</u>: The government did not release statistics on prison demographics and capacity. Some prisoners reported poor sanitary conditions, poor temperature control, and overcrowding.

There were reports in prior years that individuals within state security detention facilities were mistreated.

There was no information available on whether prisoners with HIV/AIDS received appropriate health care. Medical care was generally adequate in regular prisons, although some prisoners reported extended delays in receiving medical treatment and difficulty obtaining necessary medication. Most prisons had nurses or other medical professionals on duty, although reportedly prison doctors were often reluctant to issue anything other than nonprescription pain medication. In addition, media reports stated some detainees in State Security Department custody did not receive adequate access to medical care.

Prisons attempted to accommodate persons with disabilities based on their specific needs, such as by placing a wheelchair user on a lower floor. Some reports alleged inconsistencies in providing support for prisoners with mental disabilities. In Dubai and to some extent Abu Dhabi, prison officials worked with mental health professionals to provide support and administer needed medication. Training and capabilities to accommodate prisoners with mental health disabilities were allegedly less well developed in the other emirates. Reportedly it was common for authorities to grant a humanitarian pardon in cases where a person with a disability had been convicted of a minor offense.

Administration: Some state security detainees did not have access to visitors or had more limited access than other prisoners. Although prisoners had a right to submit complaints to judicial authorities, details about investigations into complaints were not publicly available and there were no independent authorities to investigate allegations of poor conditions. There was also no publicly available information on whether or not authorities investigated complaints about prison conditions. Dubai Emirate maintained a website where individuals could obtain basic information about pending legal cases including formal charges and upcoming court dates.

Independent Monitoring: The government permitted charitable NGOs to visit prisons and provide material support on a limited basis. Members of the government-sanctioned Emirates Human Rights Association (EHRA) met with prisoners during regular visits to detention facilities and reported their findings to federal Ministry of Interior officials. Their reports were not publicly available. Authorities did not grant regular consular access for State Security Department detainees.

d. Arbitrary Arrest or Detention

The constitution prohibits arbitrary arrest and detention; however, the government reportedly often held persons in custody for extended periods without charge or a preliminary judicial hearing. The law permits indefinite detention, including incommunicado detention, without appeal. In some cases authorities did not allow detainees contact with attorneys, family members, or others for indefinite or unspecified periods.

In cases of foreign nationals detained by police, which in view of the country's demographic breakdown were the vast majority of cases, the government often did not notify the appropriate diplomatic missions. For state security detainees, notification was exceptionally rare and information about the status of these detainees was very limited.

Authorities treated prisoners arrested for political or security reasons differently from other prisoners, including placing them in separate sections of a prison. A specific government entity, the State Security Department, handled these cases, and in some cases held prisoners and detainees in separate undisclosed locations for extended periods prior to their transfer to a regular prison.

In May, two Libyan-Americans accused of state security violations were acquitted following a Federal Supreme Court trail. The individuals were originally arrested in August 2014, but formal charges were not filed until January 2016. Also authorities did not inform their families or relevant consular missions at the time of the arrest; they were denied access to legal counsel; and they reported that they were tortured while in detention.

Role of the Police and Security Apparatus

Each emirate maintained a local police force called a general directorate, which was officially a branch of the federal Ministry of Interior. All emirate-level general directorates of police enforced their respective emirate's laws autonomously. They also enforced federal laws within their emirate in coordination with each other under the federal ministry. The federal government maintained federal armed forces for external security.

There were no public reports of impunity involving security forces, but there was no publicly available information on whether or not authorities investigated complaints of police corruption or other abuses including prison conditions and mistreatment (see section 1.c., Administration).

Arrest Procedures and Treatment of Detainees

Police stations received complaints from the public, made arrests, and forwarded cases to the public prosecutor. The public prosecutor then transferred cases to the courts. The law prohibits arrest or search of citizens without probable cause. Unlike the previous year, there were no reports security forces failed to obtain warrants. Police must report an arrest within 48 hours to the public prosecutor, and police usually adhered to the deadline.

The law requires prosecutors to submit charges to a court within 14 days of the police reporting the case to them and to inform detainees of the charges against them; however, judges may grant extensions to prosecutors, sometimes resulting in extended periods of detention without formal charges. Multiple detainees complained authorities did not inform them of charges until several days after they had been detained. Noncitizen detainees reported that when the prosecutor presented the charges, they were written in Arabic with no translation, and that authorities pressured detainees to sign a statement saying they understood the charges placed against them.

Public prosecutors may order detainees held as long as 21 days without charge; this can be extended by court order. Judges may not grant an extension of more than 30 days of detention without charge; however, they may renew 30-day extensions indefinitely. As a result, pretrial detention sometimes exceeded the maximum sentence for the crime charged. Public prosecutors may hold suspects in terrorism-related cases without charge for six months. Once authorities charge a suspect with terrorism, the Federal Supreme Court may extend the detention indefinitely.

There is no formal system of bail. Authorities may temporarily release detainees who deposit money, a passport, or an unsecured personal promissory statement signed by a third party. Authorities may deny pretrial release to defendants in cases involving loss of life, including involuntary manslaughter. Authorities released some prisoners detained on charges related to a person's death after the prisoners completed diya (blood money) payments.

A defendant is entitled to an attorney after authorities complete their investigation. Authorities sometimes questioned the accused for weeks without permitting access to an attorney. The government may provide counsel at its discretion to indigent defendants charged with felonies punishable by imprisonment of three to 15 years. The law requires the government to provide counsel in cases in which indigent defendants face punishments of life imprisonment or the death penalty.

Authorities held some persons incommunicado, particularly in cases involving state security. For example, according to human rights groups the location and status of Emirati activist Nassir bin Ghaith remained unknown from the time of his arrest in August 2015 until April, when prosecutors announced charges of defaming a foreign country (Egypt), ridiculing the UAE's decision to grant land for a Hindu temple, and having ties to Islamist groups. Bin Ghaith, who remained in prison as of year's end, was convicted in 2011 of insulting the country's leadership, incitement, and endangering national security. On December 5, his case was transferred from the State Security chamber of the Federal Supreme Court to the Federal Court of Appeal.

<u>Arbitrary Arrest</u>: There were reports the government committed arrests without informing the individual of the charge, notably in cases of alleged violations of state security regulations. In these cases, authorities did not give notice to the individual or to family members regarding the subject of the inquiry or arrest.

<u>Pretrial Detention</u>: Lengthy pretrial detention occurred, especially in cases involving state security; however, the speed at which these cases were brought to trial increased during the year with a higher number of State Security Court acquittals and convictions in comparison to the previous year. There was no estimate available of the percentage of the prison population in pretrial status.

<u>Detainee's Ability to Challenge Lawfulness of Detention before a Court</u>: There were reports that authorities sometimes delayed or limited an individual's access to an attorney, and did not give prompt court appearances or afford consular notification, particularly in state security cases. The law permits indefinite detention without appeal in state security-related cases. There were no reports of courts finding individuals to have been unlawfully detained and recommending compensation.

e. Denial of Fair Public Trial

The constitution provides for an independent judiciary; however, court decisions remained subject to review by the political leadership. Authorities often treated noncitizens differently from citizens. The judiciary consisted largely of contracted foreign nationals subject to potential deportation, further compromising its independence from the government.

Trial Procedures

The constitution provides for the right to a fair and public trial, and the judiciary generally enforced this right.

The law presumes all defendants innocent until proven guilty. By law a defendant enjoys the right to be informed promptly and in detail of the charges. The law requires all court proceedings be conducted in Arabic. Despite the defendant's procedural right to an interpreter, there were reports authorities did not always provide an interpreter or that quality was sometimes poor.

The constitution provides the right to a public trial, except in national security cases or cases the judge deems harmful to public morality. Defendants have the right to be present at their trials and have a right to legal counsel in court. While awaiting a decision on official charges at the police station or the prosecutor's office, a defendant is not entitled to legal counsel. In cases involving a capital crime or possible life imprisonment, the defendant has a right to government-provided counsel after charges have been filed. The government may also provide counsel, at its discretion, to indigent defendants charged with felonies punishable by imprisonment of three to 15 years. The law provides prosecutors discretion to bar defense counsel from any investigation. Defendants and their attorneys may present witnesses and question witnesses against them, and defense counsel has the right to access relevant government-held evidence. Defendants may not to be compelled to testify or confess. Some defendants said they did not have adequate time to prepare a defense and requested additional time, which judges typically granted.

Both local and federal courts have an appeals process; cases under local jurisdiction are appealed to the Court of Cassation and federal cases to the Federal Supreme Court. Convicted defendants may also appeal death sentences to the ruler of the emirate in which the offense was committed or to the president of the federation. In murder cases, the victim's family must consent to commute a death sentence. The government normally negotiated with victims' families for the defendant to offer diya in exchange for forgiveness and a commuted death sentence. The prosecutor may appeal acquittals and provide new or additional evidence to a higher court. An appellate court must reach unanimous agreement to overturn an acquittal.

Prior to November, state security cases were heard exclusively at the Federal Supreme Court and were therefore not subject to appeal by a higher court; however, in November the law was amended so that state security cases are now heard at the Federal Court of Appeal, and as a result can be appealed to the higher Federal Supreme Court.

When authorities suspected a foreigner of crimes of moral turpitude, authorities sometimes deported the individual without recourse to the criminal justice system.

At the judge's discretion, foreigners charged with crimes may be permitted to defend themselves while on bail.

The penal code also requires all individuals to pay diya to victims' families in cases where accidents or crimes caused the death of another person, and media reported multiple cases of courts imposing this punishment. In some cases sharia courts imposed more severe penalties during the month of Ramadan. There were also reports courts applied these punishments more strictly to Muslims.

Women faced legal discrimination because of the government's interpretation of sharia law (see section 6).

Political Prisoners and Detainees

During the year there were reports of persons held, typically incommunicado and without charge, for their political views or affiliations, often because of alleged links to Islamist organizations.

According to news reports, prosecutors brought approximately 200 state security cases to court since 2013, including about 70 during the first half of the year. Most convictions were for terrorism-related crimes or membership in banned organizations. Human rights organizations alleged that some of these cases involved individuals advocating nonviolent change, and they criticized the government for using overly broad antiterrorism laws to arrest and detain those with suspected ties to nonviolent, political Islamist movements.

In the aftermath of the Arab Spring, the government restricted the activities of organizations and individuals allegedly associated with Dawat al-Islah, a Muslim Brotherhood affiliate, and others critical of the government. Media reported two Emiratis were convicted and jailed on November 14 with 10- and seven-year jail sentences for being leading members of al-Islah.

As part of its security and counterterrorism efforts, the government issued or updated restrictive laws--such as the 2014 antiterrorism law--governing activities, including the use of the internet and social media. Numerous observers criticized these laws as extending beyond security concerns by also outlawing activities and speech of a political nature.

Civil Judicial Procedures and Remedies

Citizens and noncitizens had access to the courts to seek damages for, or cessation of, human rights violations. The civil courts, like all courts, lacked full independence. In some cases courts delayed proceedings.

f. Arbitrary or Unlawful Interference with Privacy, Family, Home, or Correspondence

The constitution prohibits entry into a home without the owner's permission, except when police present a lawful warrant. Officers' actions in searching premises were subject to review by the Ministry of Interior, and officers were subject to disciplinary action if authorities judged their actions irresponsible.

The constitution provides for freed and confidential correspondence by mail, telegram, and all other means of communication. There were reports, however, that the government monitored and in some cases censored incoming international mail and wiretapped telephones and monitored outgoing mail and electronic forms of communication without following appropriate legal procedures. A May 29 study by the University of Toronto's Citizen Lab reported that since 2012, Emirati journalists, activists, and dissidents have been targeted by sophisticated spyware attacks, which the researchers found may be linked to the Emirati government (see also section 2.a., Internet Freedom).

Local interpretation of sharia prohibits Muslim women from marrying non-Muslims and Muslim men from marrying women "not of the book," generally meaning adherents of religions other than Islam, Christianity, and Judaism.

The country employs judicial supervision for individuals considered at risk from relatives committing honor crimes against or otherwise harming them. Judicial supervision typically included housing individuals to provide for their well-being and for family mediation and reconciliation.

g. Abuses in Internal Conflict

In March 2015, in response to a request from Yemeni president Abd Rabbuh Mansour Hadi for Arab League/Gulf Cooperation Council military intervention, Saudi officials announced the formation of a coalition to counter the 2014 overthrow of the legitimate government in Yemen by militias of the Ansar Allah movement (also known colloquially as "Houthis") and forces loyal to former Yemeni president Ali Abdullah Saleh. The Saudi-led coalition, which also includes the UAE, Bahrain, Egypt, Jordan, Kuwait, Morocco, Qatar, Somalia,

Sudan, and Senegal, conducted air and ground operations that continued throughout the year. UAE forces continued an active military role in Yemen, including conducting ground operations against al-Qaeda in the Arabian Peninsula (AQAP) in Mukalla.

The UN and NGOs such as HRW and Amnesty International (AI) and some Yemeni sources have voiced human rights concerns about coalition activities in Yemen, claiming some Saudi-led coalition airstrikes have been disproportionate or indiscriminate, and appeared not to sufficiently minimize collateral impact on civilians. UAE forces have not been specifically accused of carrying out such strikes. Some Yemeni opposition-aligned press reports have also alleged coalition forces and local Yemeni forces have abducted, arbitrarily detained, and mistreated individuals, including those without apparent ties to terrorist organizations, as part of their counterterrorism efforts in the Mukalla area.

For additional details, see the Department of State's *Country Report on Human Rights* for Yemen.

Section 2. Respect for Civil Liberties, Including:

a. Freedom of Speech and Press

The constitution provides for freedom of speech and of the press; however, the law prohibits criticism of national rulers and speech that may create or encourage social unrest; the government restricted freedom of speech and press.

<u>Freedom of Speech and Expression</u>: After the onset of the Arab Spring in 2011, authorities severely restricted public criticism of the government and ministers. The government continued to make arrests or impose other restrictions for speech related to and in support of Islamist political activities, calls for democratic reforms, criticism of or perceived insults against the government and government institutions, and in rarer cases, criticism of individuals. In February a court sentenced Omani citizen Saleh Mohammed al-Awaisi to a three-year jail term for sharing a poem over social media that ridiculed the government and its soldiers in Yemen. He was tried under the cybercrime law, which criminalizes all forms of electronic abuse.

In another case, in January authorities issued an arrest warrant for two men who had posted a video of themselves in military uniforms, mimicking the dance moves from a popular Saudi music video. The authorities accused the men of dishonoring the country's military services. Also in January, the Federal Supreme Court sentenced Mohammed Ashour to three years in prison for creating a Facebook page that allegedly damaged the reputation of the country. In other cases, authorities brought individuals to trial for posting material on social media platforms that was seen as personally insulting to acquaintances, colleagues, employers, or religions.

Press and Media Freedoms: International NGOs categorized the press, both in print and online, as not free. Except for media outlets located in Dubai and Abu Dhabi's free trade zones, the government owned most newspapers, television stations, and radio stations. All media conformed to unpublished government reporting guidelines. The government also influenced the privately owned media, through the National Media Council (NMC), which directly oversaw all media content. Satellite-receiving dishes were widespread and provided access to uncensored international broadcasts.

In February, Jordanian media outlets and human rights groups reported that Jordanian journalist Tayseer al-Najjar had been detained in mid-December 2015 without charge and was being held incommunicado. His wife subsequently told the press that authorities had accused him of spying for Qatar, criticizing the UAE, and criticizing Egyptian President Abdel Fattah al-Sisi. Human Rights Watch reported in December that al-Najjar was transferred to al-Wathba prison in March and had not been provided with access to legal counsel or informed of the charges against him. Al-Najjar remained in detention at year's end.

Censorship or Content Restrictions: By law the NMC, whose members the president appoints, licenses and censors all publications, including private association publications. The law authorizes censorship of domestic and foreign publications to remove criticism of the government, ruling families, or friendly governments; statements that "threaten social stability;" and materials considered pornographic, excessively violent, derogatory to Islam, or supportive of certain Israeli government positions. The law also criminalizes, as blasphemy, acts that provoke religious hatred or insult religious convictions through any form of expression, including broadcasting, printed media, or the internet.

According to the NMC and Dubai police officials, authorities did not give journalists specific instructions; however, government officials reportedly warned journalists when they published or broadcast material deemed politically or culturally sensitive. Journalists commonly practiced self-censorship due to fear of government retribution, particularly since most journalists were foreign nationals and could be deported. Authorities did not allow some books perceived as critical of the government, Islam, and Emirati culture, as well as books that supported the Muslim Brotherhood or its ideology.

Libel/Slander Laws: The government used libel and slander laws to suppress criticism of its leaders and institutions. The law criminalizes acts that defame others through online or information technology means. Those who commit libel may face up to two years in prison; the maximum penalty for those convicted of libel against the family of a public official is three years in prison.

In May the courts convicted three sports journalists of slander and handed each a three-month suspended prison sentence after they publicly criticized a competitor television channel.

National Security: Authorities often cited the need to protect national security as the basis for laws that curb criticism of government or expression of dissenting political views. For example, the country's cybercrimes laws include broad limitations on using electronic means to promote disorder or "damage national unity." Human rights groups criticized these laws for excessively restricting freedom of speech.

Internet Freedom

The government restricted access to some websites and monitored social media, instant messaging services, and blogs. Authorities stated they could imprison individuals for misusing the internet. Self-censorship was apparent on social media, and there were reports the Ministry of Interior monitored internet use. The International Telecommunication Union estimated more than 90 percent of the population had access to the internet.

The country's two internet service providers, both linked to the government, used a proxy server to block materials deemed inconsistent with the country's values, as defined by the Ministry of Interior. Blocked material included pornographic websites and a wide variety of other sites deemed indecent, as well as those dealing with lesbian, gay, bisexual, transgender, and intersex (LGBTI) issues; Judaism and atheism; negative critiques of Islam; testimonies of former Muslims who converted to Christianity; gambling; promotion of illegal drug use; and postings that explained how to circumvent the proxy servers. International media sites accessed using the country's internet providers contained filtered content. The government also blocked some sites that contained content critical of ruling families in the

UAE and other states in the region. The Telecommunications Regulatory Authority was responsible for creating lists of blocked sites. Service providers did not have the authority to remove sites from blocked lists without government approval. The government also blocked most voice-over-internet-protocol applications. In June authorities asked Snapchat to block content after some users complained to the telecoms regulator of objectionable content. Also in June, authorities blocked the website of news organization Middle East Eye.

The law explicitly criminalizes use of the internet to commit a wide variety of offenses and provides fines and prison terms for internet users who violate political, social, and religious norms. The law provides penalties for using the internet to oppose Islam; to proselytize Muslims to join other religions; to abuse a holy shrine or ritual of any religion; to insult any religion, belief, sect, race, color, or ethnic group; to incite someone to commit sin; or to contravene family values by publishing news or photographs pertaining to a person's private life or family. In February the government announced it would increase fines and jail terms for the "criminal intent" use of Virtual Private Networks, which often were used to circumvent internet censorship.

In August news reports alleged that authorities had used a malware application to obtain access to the iPhone of Emirati political activist Ahmed Mansoor by exploiting a flaw in Apple's iOS operating system.

The 2012 cybercrimes decree and the 2015 Antidiscrimination Law provide for more severe penalties for violations and add to existing online communication limitations on freedom of speech to include prohibitions on criticism or defamation of the government or its officials; insults based on religion, belief, sect, race, color, or ethnic origin; insults directed at neighboring countries; and calls for protests and demonstrations.

Academic Freedom and Cultural Events

The government restricted academic freedom, including speech both inside and outside the classroom by educators, and censored academic materials for schools. The government required official permission for conferences and submission of detailed information on proposed speakers and topics of discussion. Some organizations found it difficult to secure meeting space for public events that dealt with contentious issues.

Cultural institutions avoided displaying artwork or programming that criticized the government or religion. Self-censorship among cultural and other institutions, especially for content presented to the public, was pervasive and generally directed at preventing the appearance of illegal works, including those deemed as promoting blasphemy or addressing controversial political issues.

b. Freedom of Peaceful Assembly and Association

The constitution provides for the freedoms of assembly and association; however, the government did not always respect these rights.

Freedom of Assembly

The law provides limited freedom of assembly and the government imposed restrictions.

The law requires a government-issued permit for organized public gatherings. Authorities dispersed impromptu protests such as labor strikes and at times arrested participants. While there was no uniform standard for the number of persons who could gather without a permit, civil society representatives in the past have reported authorities could ask groups of four or more to disperse if they did not have a permit. The government did not interfere routinely with informal, nonpolitical gatherings held without a government permit in public places unless there were complaints. The government generally permitted political gatherings that supported its policies. Hotels, citing government regulations, sometimes denied permission for groups such as religious organizations to rent space for meetings or religious services.

Freedom of Association

The law provides limited freedom of association. The government imposed some restrictions.

Political organizations, political parties, and trade unions are illegal. All associations and NGOs are required to register with the Ministry of Social Affairs, and many that did received government subsidies. Domestic NGOs registered with the ministry were mostly citizens' associations for economic, religious, social, cultural, athletic, and other purposes. Registration rules require that all voting organizational members, as well as boards of directors, must be Emirati; this excluded almost 90 percent of the population from fully participating in such organizations.

Associations must follow the government's censorship guidelines and receive prior government approval before publishing any material. In Abu Dhabi, exhibitions, conferences, and meetings require a permit from the Tourism and Culture Authority. To obtain a permit, the event organizer must submit identification documents for speakers along with speaker topics; the government denied permits if it did not approve of the topic or speaker.

c. Freedom of Religion

See the Department of State's *International Religious Freedom Report* at www.state.gov/religiousfreedomreport/.

d. Freedom of Movement, Internally Displaced Persons, Protection of Refugees, and Stateless Persons

The law generally provided for freedom of internal movement, emigration, and repatriation, and the government generally respected these rights; however, the government imposed certain legal restrictions on foreign travel. The government allowed the Office of the UN High Commissioner for Refugees (UNHCR) and other humanitarian organizations to provide protection and assistance to refugees, asylum seekers, stateless persons, and other persons of concern. The lack of passports or other identity documents restricted the movement of stateless persons, both within the country and internationally.

Foreign Travel: Authorities generally did not permit citizens and residents involved in legal disputes under adjudication, and noncitizens under investigation to travel abroad. In addition, authorities sometimes arrested individuals with outstanding debts or legal cases while in transit through an airport.

At the sole discretion of emirate-level prosecutors, foreign nationals had their passports taken or travel restricted during criminal and civil investigations, which in some cases times posed significant difficulties. Some were also banned from foreign travel. These measures posed particular problems for noncitizen debtors, who in addition to being unable to leave the country, were usually unable to find work without a passport and valid residence permit, and as a result were unable to repay their debts or maintain legal residency.

Travel bans could also be placed on citizens; citizens of interest for reasons of state security, including former political prisoners, also encountered difficulties renewing official documents, resulting in de facto travel bans.

Authorities did not lift travel bans until the completion of a case in the judicial system. In complex cases, particularly in the investigation of financial crimes, travel bans remained in place for three years or more.

Custom dictates that a husband may prevent his wife, minor children, and adult unmarried daughters from leaving the country by taking custody of their passports.

Citizenship: The government may revoke naturalized citizens' passports and citizenship status for criminal or politically provocative actions. According to AI, in March authorities confiscated the passports and revoked the citizenship of three siblings whose father had been convicted previously of membership in Al Islah, a group the government designated as a terrorist organization.

Protection of Refugees

UNHCR lacked formal legal status in the country separate from the UN Development Program; however, the government worked with UNHCR on a case-by-case basis to address refugee issues. The government did not formally grant refugee status or asylum to aliens seeking protection; however, it allowed some refugees to remain in the country temporarily on an individual basis. This nonpermanent status often presented administrative, financial, and social hardships, including the need frequently to renew visas and the inability to access basic services such as health care and education for children.

Access to Asylum: The law does not provide for the granting of asylum or refugee status, and the government had not established a transparent, codified system for providing protection to refugees. While the government extended informal protection from return to refugees in some cases, any persons lacking legal residency status were technically subject to local laws on illegal immigrants and authorities could detain them. There were no reports, however, that the government sent individuals who expressed a fear of return back to their country of origin against their will. In some cases authorities confined individuals seeking protection at an airport to a specific section of the airport while they awaited resettlement in another country.

<u>Access to Basic Services</u>: Access to employment, education, and other public services, including health care, is based on an individual's status as a legal resident. Persons with a claim to refugee status, including those with either short-term visitor visas or expired visas, were generally not eligible for such benefits, and as a result some families, particularly from Iraq and Syria, reportedly did not have access to healthcare or school for children. The government provided or allowed access to some services on a case-by-case basis, often after the intervention of UNHCR representatives.

Stateless Persons

Estimates suggested 20,000 to 100,000 bidoon, or persons without citizenship, resided in the country. Most bidoon lacked citizenship because they did not have the preferred tribal affiliation used to determine citizenship when the country was established. Others entered the country legally or illegally in search of employment. Because children derive citizenship generally from the father, bidoon children born within the country's territory remained stateless. Without passports or other forms of identification, the movement of bidoon was restricted, both within the country and internationally.

The government has a naturalization process, and individuals may apply for citizenship. Children of female citizens married to noncitizens do not acquire citizenship automatically at birth, but their mothers may obtain citizenship for the children after submitting an application, which a government committee reviews and generally accepts, once the child is 18 years old. A foreign woman may receive citizenship after 10 years of marriage to a citizen. Anyone may receive a passport by presidential fiat.

The committee that reviews mothers' citizenship applications for their children also reviews citizenship applications from bidoon who could satisfy certain legal conditions to be eligible for naturalization and subsequently could gain access to education, health care, and other public services. There were no reports, however, of stateless persons receiving Emirati citizenship.

Section 3. Freedom to Participate in the Political Process

The law does not provide citizens the ability to choose their government in free and fair periodic elections based on universal and equal suffrage and conducted by secret ballot guaranteeing the free expression of the will of the people. Federal executive and legislative power is in the hands of the Federal Supreme Council, a body composed of the hereditary rulers of the seven emirates. It selects from its members the country's president and vice president. Decisions at the federal level generally are by consensus among the rulers, their families, and other leading families. The ruling families, in consultation with other prominent tribal figures, also choose rulers of the emirates.

Citizens could express their concerns directly to their leaders through an open majlis, a traditional consultative mechanism. On occasion women attended a majlis. If a majlis was closed to women, men sometimes voiced concerns as proxies on behalf of women. In addition, authorities sometimes held a women-only majlis or a majlis focused specifically on women's issues.

Elections and Political Participation

Recent Elections: There were no democratic general elections. In October 2015 an appointed electorate of more than 224,000 members, representing approximately one-fifth of the total citizen population, elected 20 members of the FNC, a 40-member consultative body with some legislative authority. Each emirate receives seats in the FNC based on population. Each emirate's ruler appoints that emirate's portion of the other 20 FNC members. The electorate appointment process lacked transparency. Approximately 35 percent of eligible voters participated, electing one woman among the 20 FNC members, with another eight women appointed by their respective rulers. The speaker of the FNC, appointed in November 2015, is the first woman to lead the FNC.

Political Parties and Political Participation: Citizens did not have the right to form political parties. There were no reports of citizens attempting to form political parties.

Participation of Women and Minorities: Although some traditional practices discouraged women from engaging in political life, the government prioritized women's participation in government. There were eight female ministers in the 24-member cabinet, and nine women (one elected, who was appointed speaker) in the FNC.

Except in the judiciary and military, religious and racial minorities (including Shia) did not serve in senior federal positions. Many judges were contracted foreign nationals.

Section 4. Corruption and Lack of Transparency in Government

The law provides criminal penalties for official corruption, and the government generally implemented the law effectively. There were isolated reports of government corruption.

Nepotism and conflict of interest in government appointments and contract allocations existed. The Ministries of the Interior and Justice and the state audit institutions are responsible for combating government corruption.

Corruption: In August, Khadem al-Qubaisi, the former head of one of the country's primary sovereign wealth funds, was arrested following allegations of wide-scale financial fraud. The authorities reportedly had frozen the travel documents of Qubaisi and a second senior executive in April as part of a money laundering and embezzlement investigation.

Authorities also prosecuted cases of police corruption. In June, Dubai authorities brought a police officer to court, accusing him of accepting a bribe to release a prisoner he was transporting.

Financial Disclosure: There are no financial disclosure laws, regulations, or codes of conduct requiring officials to disclose their income and assets. The operating instructions for the Federal National Council elections did require all candidates to disclose sources of funding for their campaigns.

Public Access to Information: The law provides for public access to government information, but the government followed this provision selectively. Requests for access usually went unanswered. There were no reports of public outreach activities or training for public officials to encourage the effective use of the law to access public information.

Section 5. Governmental Attitude Regarding International and Nongovernmental Investigation of Alleged Violations of Human Rights

The government generally did not permit organizations to focus on domestic political issues. Two recognized local human rights organizations existed: the government-supported EHRA, which focused on human rights problems and complaints on matters such as labor conditions, stateless persons' rights, and prisoners' well-being and treatment; and the government-subsidized Emirates Association for Lawyers and Legal Council (formerly the Jurists' Association Human Rights Administration), which focused on human rights education and conducted seminars and symposia subject to government approval. Several EHRA members worked in the government and the organization received government funding. The EHRA viewed itself as operating independently without government interference, apart from the requirements that apply to all associations in the country.

The government directed, regulated, and subsidized participation by all NGO members in events outside the country. All participants must obtain government permission before attending such events. The government also restricted entry to the country by members of international NGOs. The 2015 Antidiscrimination Law provides a legal basis for restricting events such as conferences and seminars.

The United Nations or Other International Bodies: The government did not allow international human rights NGOs to be based in the country but, on a limited basis, allowed representatives to visit. There were no transparent standards governing visits from international NGO representatives.

Section 6. Discrimination, Societal Abuses, and Trafficking in Persons

Women

Rape and Domestic Violence: The law criminalizes rape, which is punishable by death under the penal code. The penal code does not address spousal rape. The penal code allows men to use physical means, including violence, at their discretion against female and minor family members. Punishments issued by courts in domestic abuse cases were often minimal. In some cases, police shared a victim's contact information with her/his family, which sometimes reached the assailant. The Dubai Foundation for Women and Children managed a shelter in Dubai for domestic abuse victims and was active in increasing awareness of domestic violence problems and avenues available for victims to seek help. For the first half of the year the organization reported 196 cases of domestic violence.

In general the government did not enforce domestic abuse laws effectively, and domestic abuse against women, including spousal abuse, remained a problem. There were reports employers raped or sexually assaulted foreign domestic workers. These cases rarely went to court, and those that did led to few convictions. In sharia courts, which are primarily responsible for civil matters between Muslims, the extremely high burden of proof for a rape case contributed to a low conviction rate. Additionally, female victims of rape or other sexual crimes faced the possibility of prosecution for consensual sex outside marriage instead of receiving assistance from authorities.

Victims of domestic abuse may file complaints with police units stationed in major public hospitals. Social workers and counselors, usually female, also maintained offices in public hospitals and police stations. Women, however, often were reluctant to file formal charges of abuse for social, cultural, and economic reasons. There were domestic abuse centers in Abu Dhabi, Dubai, Ras al-Khaimah, and Sharjah.

The government, in coordination with social organizations, sought to increase awareness of domestic violence, conducting seminars, educational programs, symposiums, and conferences. The Dubai Foundation for Women and Children increased awareness of domestic violence through social media, television and radio programming and advertising, by hosting workshops, and by sponsoring a hotline. The organization also offered services to all those residing in or transiting the country, including legal services and rehabilitation programs.

Female Genital Mutilation/Cutting (FGM/C): The law does not address FGM/C, although the Ministry of Health prohibits hospitals and clinics from performing the procedure. The practice was rare and confined to foreign residents.

Sexual Harassment: The government prosecutes harassment via the penal code. Conviction of "disgracing or dishonoring" a person in public is punishable by a minimum of one year and up to 15 years in prison if the victim is under age 14. Conviction for "infamous" acts against the rules of decency is punishable by a penalty of six months in prison, and "dishonoring a woman by word or deed on a public roadway" is also a punishable offense.

Reproductive Rights: Married couples have the right to decide freely the number, spacing, and timing of their children; have the information and means to do so; and have the right to attain the highest standard of reproductive health free from discrimination, coercion, and violence. Authorities typically deported unmarried noncitizen workers who become pregnant. Hospitals do not issue birth certificates to children born to unmarried parents, making it difficult for a child to remain in the country or to obtain the necessary documents, such as a passport, to depart. Abortion is generally illegal; however, it is allowed if the pregnancy endangers the life of the mother. The government provides free healthcare to citizens, including access to contraception, obstetric and gynecologic services, prenatal care, and delivery care to married female citizens. Despite this, only 39 percent of women aged 15-49 used a modern method of contraceptives, and 20 percent of women had an unmet need for planning, according to UN Population Fund 2015 estimates. The government did not provide free antenatal care for noncitizen pregnant women.

<u>Discrimination</u>: Women in general faced legal and economic discrimination, with noncitizen women at particular disadvantage. The treatment of Emirati women showed some signs of improvement.

The government's interpretation of sharia applies in personal status cases and family law. As noted above, the law forbids Muslim women to marry non-Muslims.

In addition, the law permits a man to have as many as four wives; women normally inherit less than men; and a son may inheritance may be double what a daughter's.

For a woman to obtain a divorce with a financial settlement, she must prove her husband inflicted physical or moral harm upon her, abandoned her for at least three months, or had not provided her or their children's upkeep. Alternatively, women may divorce by paying compensation or surrendering their dowry to their husbands. Strict interpretation of sharia does not apply to child custody cases, as courts have applied the "the best interests of the child" standard since 2010.

The law provides for corporal punishment for sexual relations and pregnancy outside of marriage. The government may imprison and deport noncitizen women if they bear children out of wedlock. In previous years, authorities arrested some victims of sexual assault for sexual relations outside of marriage.

Women who worked in the private sector regularly did not receive equal benefits and reportedly faced discrimination in promotions and pay (see section 7.d.).

While foreign men working in the country and earning a salary above a certain level could obtain residency permits for their families for three years, a foreign woman could obtain a one year, renewable permit for her family only if she was working in a job deemed rare or with a specialty such as health care, engineering, or teaching.

While education is equally accessible, federal law prohibits coeducation in public schools and universities, except in the United Arab Emirates University's Executive MBA program and in certain graduate programs at Zayed University. A large number of private schools, private universities, and institutions, however, were coeducational. Women hold two-thirds of public sector posts, including 30 percent of senior and decision-making positions, according to government estimates.

The government excluded women from certain social benefits including land grants for building houses because tribal family law often designates men as the heads of families.

The government has a Gender Balance Council to promote a greater role for female citizens, but not noncitizens, who were working outside the home. Its activities primarily focused on speaking and awareness raising activities including seminars, workshops, and conferences aimed at educating and empowering women. The government requires female participation on the boards of government agencies and companies.

Children

Birth Registration: Children derive citizenship generally from their parents. As noted, the children of Emirati mothers married to foreigners did not receive citizenship automatically. The government registered noncitizen births, including of bidoon.

Education: Education is compulsory through the ninth grade; however, the law was not enforced, and some children did not attend school, especially children of noncitizens. Noncitizen children could enroll in public schools only if they scored more than 90 percent on entrance examinations, which authorities administered only in Arabic. The government provided free primary education only to citizens. Public schools are not coeducational after kindergarten. Islamic studies are mandatory in all public schools and in private schools serving Muslim students.

Child Abuse: The law prohibits child abuse and the government has taken steps to increase awareness of the issue. The government provided shelter and help for child victims of abuse or sexual exploitation. Newspapers frequently advertised the Ministry of Interior's child abuse reporting hotline and carried stories of prosecutions of child abuse cases. In June the government enacted a new Child Rights Law that included increased reporting requirements for suspected cases of child abuse, tightened definitions of abuse, and increased legal punishments.

<u>Early and Forced Marriage</u>: The legal age of marriage for both men and women is 18.

<u>Sexual Exploitation of Children</u>: The law criminalizes the sexual exploitation of children, with a minimum penalty for conviction of 10 years in prison. Consensual sex is illegal outside of marriage, carrying a minimum penalty of one year in prison. The penalty for conviction of sex with children under age 14 is life imprisonment. Distribution and consumption of child pornography is illegal.

<u>International Child Abductions</u>: The country is not a party to the 1980 Hague Convention on the Civil Aspects of International Child Abduction. See the Department of State's *Annual Report on International Parental Child Abduction* at travel.state.gov/content/childabduction/en/legal/compliance.html.

Anti-Semitism

There is no indigenous Jewish community. There were no synagogues and no formal recognition for the very small foreign Jewish population (which constituted less than 1 percent of the population); the foreign Jewish community could conduct regular prayer services in rented space. Occasionally social media contained anti-Semitic remarks, and there was anti-Semitic material available at some book fairs including a few that operated with government oversight.

Trafficking in Persons

See the Department of State's *Trafficking in Persons Report* at www.state.gov/j/tip/rls/tiprpt/.

Persons with Disabilities

The law prohibits discrimination against persons who have physical, sensory, intellectual, and mental disabilities in employment, education, air travel and other transportation, access to health care, or the provision of other state services; however, some discrimination occurred.

Public and private facilities provided education, health services, sports, and vocational rehabilitation for persons with disabilities; however, capacity was insufficient. Many of the facilities were reserved for citizens. There were reports that in some cases authorities detained individuals for behavior linked to a mental disability, rather than send them to a medical facility. These individuals were later acquitted because of their disabilities.

The Ministry of Social Affairs is the central body dealing with the rights of persons with disabilities and raising awareness at the federal and local level. In accordance with the law, most public buildings provided some form of access for persons with disabilities.

Government entities, including the Ministry of Social Affairs, the Services for Educational Development Foundation for Inclusion, and the Sports Organizations for Persons with Disabilities, sponsored conferences and workshops emphasizing the inclusion and integration of persons with disabilities into schools and workplaces. The Ministry of Social Affairs, which ran a number of rehabilitation centers, stated that the increased emphasis in recent years on integrating children with disabilities into regular schools opened up space in their rehabilitation centers to better accommodate persons with more significant disabilities.

Various departments within the Ministries of Labor, Education, and Social Affairs are responsible for protecting the rights of persons with disabilities, and the government enforced these rights in employment, housing, and entitlement programs. While enforcement was effective for jobs in the public sector, the government did not sufficiently encourage hiring in the private sector. The emirate of Abu Dhabi reserved 2 percent of government jobs for citizens with disabilities, and other emirates and the federal government included statements in their human resources regulations emphasizing priority for hiring citizens with disabilities in the public sector. Public sector employers provided reasonable accommodations, defined broadly, for employees with disabilities. The employment of persons with disabilities in the private sector remained a challenge due to a lack of training and opportunities, and societal discrimination.

The government sponsored several initiatives to host international conferences for persons with disabilities emphasizing rights, opportunities, and the importance of social inclusion. The government also worked to improve the accessibility of public facilities. For example in June, Dubai launched a $2.7 million study to identify specific targets and methodologies to improve accessibility for schools, hospitals, parks, and transportation facilities.

The General Authority of Sports and Youth Welfare and the Disabled Sports Federation provided programs to promote the inclusion of persons with disabilities in sporting activities.

National/Racial/Ethnic Minorities

Approximately 89 percent of the country's residents were noncitizens, more than half of whom originated from the Indian subcontinent. Societal discrimination against noncitizens was prevalent and occurred in most areas of daily life, including employment, education, housing, social interaction, and health care.

The law allows for criminalizing commercial disputes and bankruptcy, which led to discrimination against foreigners. Authorities enforced these laws selectively and allowed citizens to threaten noncitizen businesspersons and foreign workers with harsh prison sentences to assure a favorable outcome in commercial disputes. Under the penal code, those who issue checks with an insufficient account balance are punishable by detention or fine (see also section 2.d., Foreign Travel). By presidential decree citizens have immunity from prosecution for bounced checks.

Acts of Violence, Discrimination, and Other Abuses Based on Sexual Orientation and Gender Identity

Both civil law and sharia criminalize consensual same-sex sexual activity. Under sharia individuals who engage in consensual same-sex sexual conduct could be subject to the death penalty. Dubai's penal code allows for up to a 10-year prison sentence for conviction of such activity. There were no reports of arrests or prosecutions for consensual same-sex activity. In September authorities passed Federal Decree No. 4, which permits doctors to conduct sexual reassignment surgery so long as there are "psychological" and "physiological" signs of gender and sex disparity.

There were reports of LGBTI persons being questioned in Dubai airport. For example, in August media reported that authorities detained a Canadian model, allegedly on account of discrepancies between her female physical appearance and her insistence she was female, and the information contained in her passport, which authorities said contained a picture that appeared male and listed her sex as male. Due to social conventions and potential repression, LGBTI organizations did not operate openly, nor were gay pride marches or gay rights advocacy events held. Information was not available on official or private discrimination in employment, occupation, housing, statelessness, or access to education or health care based on sexual orientation and gender identity. There were no government efforts to address potential discrimination.

By law wearing clothing deemed inappropriate for one's sex is a punishable offense. The government deported foreign residents and referred the cases of individuals who wore clothing deemed inappropriate to the public prosecutor. For example, in February authorities arrested, fined, and deported a male foreign national for wearing makeup and women's clothing in a Dubai mall.

HIV and AIDS Social Stigma

Noncitizens and, to a lesser extent, citizens, with HIV/AIDS and other diseases faced discrimination. Legal protections regarding employment and education discrimination against individuals with HIV/AIDS, as well as free access to HIV treatment and care programs, existed for citizens; however, noncitizens did not have these rights. The government does not grant residency or work visas to persons with certain communicable diseases including HIV/AIDS, tuberculosis, or leprosy. Noncitizens that test positive for these diseases may be detained and deported. Doctors are required to inform authorities of HIV/AIDS cases, reportedly discouraging individuals from seeking testing or treatment. A study released in February and conducted across eight universities indicated that 85 percent of citizen students expressed negative attitudes towards those with HIV/AIDS.

Section 7. Worker Rights

a. Freedom of Association and the Right to Collective Bargaining

The law does not protect the right to organize, strike, or bargain collectively. The law does not permit workers to form or join unions. The labor law forbids strikes by public sector employees, security guards, and migrant workers. The law does not entirely prohibit strikes in the private sector, but allows an employer to suspend an employee for striking. In the private sector the Ministry of Human Resources and Emiratisation (MOHRE), formerly the Labor Ministry, must approve and register individual employment contracts. Labor law does not apply to domestic and agricultural workers or to most workers in export processing zones.

Private sector employees may file collective employment dispute complaints with the MOHRE, which by law acts as mediator between the parties. Employees may then file unresolved disputes within the labor court system, which forwards disputes to a conciliation council. Public sector employees may file an administrative grievance or a case in a civil court to address a labor-related dispute or complaint. Administrative remedies are available for labor complaints, and authorities commonly applied them to resolve issues such as delayed wage payments, unpaid overtime, or substandard housing.

All foreign workers have the right to file labor-related grievances with the MOHRE. The ministry sometimes intervened in foreign workers' disputes with employers and helped negotiate private settlements. The law allows employers to request the government to cancel the work permit of, and deport for up to one year any foreign worker for unexcused absences of more than seven days or for participating in a strike.

The government generally enforced labor law. In May, the MOHRE issued its first Worker Welfare Report, which will be updated on an annual basis, and which outlines and provides statistics on the ministry's enforcement and dispute settlement activities regarding recruitment, contract integrity, payment of wages and overtime, housing accommodation, and health and safety.

Professional associations were not independent, and authorities had broad powers to interfere in their activities. For example, the MOHRE had to license and approve professional associations, which were required to receive government approval for international affiliations and travel by members. The government granted some professional associations with majority citizen membership a limited ability to raise work-related issues, petition the government for redress, and file grievances with the government.

Foreign workers may belong to local professional associations; however, they do not have voting rights and may not serve on association boards. Apart from these professional associations, in a few instances some foreign workers came together to negotiate with their employers on issues such as housing conditions, nonpayment of wages, and working conditions.

The threat of deportation discouraged noncitizens from voicing work-related grievances. Nonetheless, occasional protests and strikes took place. The government did not always punish workers for nonviolent protests or strikes, but it dispersed such protests, and sometimes deported noncitizen participants. In July media sources reported that an estimated 1,300 workers had engaged in a strike and demonstrations in Ajman accusing their company of delays in salary payments. Workers returned to their jobs after local police and the MOHRE officials intervened to broker an agreement to pay back wages.

b. Prohibition of Forced or Compulsory Labor

The law prohibits all forms of forced or compulsory labor; however, the government did not effectively enforce the law, particularly in the domestic labor sector.

The government took steps to prevent forced labor through continued implementation of the Wages Protection System (WPS) (see section 7.e.). The government enforced fines for employers who entered incorrect information into the WPS, did not pay workers for more than 60 days, or made workers sign documents falsely attesting to receipt of benefits.

In January the government implemented three new decrees that aim to ensure that work is performed on a voluntary basis throughout the employment relationship. The first decree addresses contract substitution after arrival in the country by requiring a migrant worker to sign an offer letter in his or her home country, which is turned into a contract when the individual arrives in the UAE. The second decree addresses ending the employment relationship, allowing either party to do so subject to certain requirements of notice and/or indemnification. The third decree addresses an employee's ability to switch employers without the consent of the current employer.

It was relatively common for employers to subject migrant domestic workers, and to a lesser degree, construction and other manual labor workers, to conditions indicative of forced labor. Workers experienced nonpayment of wages, unpaid overtime, failure to grant legally required time off, withholding of passports, threats and in some cases psychological, physical, or sexual abuse. In a few cases, physical abuses led to death. Local newspapers reported on court cases involving violence committed against maids and other domestic workers. For example, in January police arrested a noncitizen woman in Dubai for killing her maid. Prosecutors said the victim had suffered multiple forms of physical abuse prior to death.

In violation of the law, employers routinely held employees' passports, thus restricting their freedom of movement and ability to leave the country or change jobs. In labor camps, it was common practice for passports to be kept in a central secure location, accessible with 24 or 48 hours' notice. In most cases, individuals reported they were able to obtain documents without difficulty when needed; however, this was not always the case. With domestic employees, passport withholding frequently occurred, and enforcement against this practice was weak.

Some employers forced foreign workers in the domestic and agricultural sectors to compensate them for hiring expenses such as visa fees, health exams, and insurance, which the law requires employers to pay, by providing unpaid labor or having these costs deducted from their contracted salary. Some employers did not pay their employees contracted wages even after they satisfied these "debts."

Though illegal, workers in both the corporate and domestic sectors often borrowed money to pay recruiting fees in their home countries, and as a result spent most of their salaries trying to repay home-country labor recruiters or lenders. These debts limited workers options to leave a job, and sometimes trapped them in exploitive work conditions. In May the country hosted the Abu Dhabi Dialogue, a forum to improve cooperation between origin and destination countries. The agenda included discussion on enhancing efforts to counter labor-recruiting abuses. In December, the government transferred oversight of recruitment of domestic workers from the interior ministry to the MOHRE.

Also see the Department of State's annual *Trafficking in Persons Report* at www.state.gov/j/tip/rls/tiprpt/.

c. Prohibition of Child Labor and Minimum Age for Employment

The law prohibits employment of persons under age 15 and includes special provisions regarding children ages 15 to 18. The law, however, excludes domestic and agricultural work, leaving underage workers in these sectors unprotected. In June the government announced a law to allow issuance of work permits for 12- to 18-year olds, specifically for gaining work experience and under specific rules. There are separate provisions regarding foreign resident children age 16 or older. The MOHRE is responsible for enforcing the regulations and generally did so effectively; violations were uncommon.

d. Discrimination with Respect to Employment and Occupation

The 2015 Antidiscrimination Law prohibits all forms of discrimination based on religion, ethnicity, or race, although without specific reference to employment. Penalties are adequate and include fines and jail terms of six months to 10 years. To date, the law has been applied in cases of religious discrimination, including one incident that occurred in a work environment.

No specific law prohibits or regulates discrimination regarding sex, political opinion, national origin or citizenship, social origin, disability, sexual orientation or gender identity, age, language, or communicable disease status in employment or occupation; however, the country is a signatory to the UN Convention on the Elimination of All Forms of Discrimination Against Women and of the International Convention on the Elimination of All Forms of Racial Discrimination. It also ratified the International Labor Organization's discrimination convention and thus submits regular reports to it on its implementation of that convention. Women who worked in the private sector, however, regularly did not receive equal benefits and reportedly faced discrimination in promotions and equality of wages. In free zones, individualized laws govern employment requirements. For example, in the Dubai International Financial Center, employers may not discriminate against any person based on sex, marital status, race, national identity, religion, or disability. Nevertheless, job advertisements requesting applications only from certain nationalities were common and not regulated.

e. Acceptable Conditions of Work

There is no minimum wage. There was very limited information on average domestic, agricultural, or construction worker salaries or on public sector salaries.

The law prescribes a 48-hour workweek and paid annual holidays. The law states daily working hours must not exceed eight hours in the day or night shifts and provides for overtime pay to employees working more than eight hours in a 24-hour period.

Government occupational health and safety standards require that employers provide employees with a safe work and living environment, including minimum rest periods and limits on the number of hours worked, depending on the nature of the work. For example, the law mandates a two-and-one-half-hour midday work break, from 12:30 p.m. to 3:00 p.m., between June 15 and September 15, for laborers who work in open areas such as construction sites. The government may exempt companies from the midday work break if the company cannot postpone the project for emergency or technical reasons. Such projects include laying asphalt or concrete and repairing damaged water pipes, gas lines, or electrical lines. The MOHRE was responsible for enforcing laws governing acceptable conditions of work for workers in semiskilled and professional job categories but did not do so in all sectors, including the informal sector and the domestic labor sector. To monitor the private sector, the ministry had active departments for inspection, occupational safety, combating human trafficking, and wage protection. The ministry published statistics on its inspection and enforcement activities.

Workers in domestic services, agriculture, and other categories overseen by the Ministry of Interior come under a different regulatory regime. These workers are not covered by private and public sector labor law, but have some legal protections regarding working hours, overtime, timeliness of wage payments, paid leave, health care, and provision of adequate housing; however, enforcement of these rules was often weak. As a result, these workers were more vulnerable to unacceptable work conditions.

There was no information available on the informal economy, or legal enforcement within this sector, or an estimate of its size; however, anecdotal reports indicate it was common for individuals to enter the country on a nonwork visa and join the informal job sector.

The MOHRE conducted inspections of labor camps and workplaces such as construction sites. The government also routinely fined employers for violating the midday break rule and published compliance statistics.

The government took action to address wage payment issues. Its implementation of the WPS and fines for noncompliance discouraged employers from withholding salaries to foreign workers under the jurisdiction of the MOHRE. The WPS, an electronic salary transfer system, requires institutions to pay workers via approved banks, exchange bureaus, and other financial institutions, to assure timely and full payment of agreed wages. The MOHRE monitored these payments electronically. The WPS, however, did not apply to foreign workers under the authority of the Ministry of Interior, such as domestic and agricultural workers.

The MOHRE conducted site visits to monitor the payment of overtime. Violations resulted in fines and in many cases a suspension of permits to hire new workers. In October, the MOHRE said that its salary enforcement efforts year to date, which included 2,200 site visits, resulted in finding violations at 122 facilities. These efforts also resulted in resolving compensation shortfalls, such as unpaid overtime and salary delays, for over 10,000 workers. According to MOHRE, it has also referred approximately 250 companies to public prosecutors for failure to pay sufficient overtime over the last five years.

The MOHRE continued efforts to ensure adequate health standards, safe food, and facilities in labor camps. It conducted regular inspections of health and living conditions at labor camps and stated that it issued written documentation on problems needing correction and reviewed them in subsequent inspections.

Nevertheless, some low-wage foreign workers faced substandard living conditions, including overcrowded apartments or unsafe and unhygienic lodging in labor camps. In some cases the ministry cancelled hiring permits for companies that failed to provide adequate housing. During some inspections of labor camps, the ministry employed interpreters to assist foreign workers in understanding employment guidelines. The ministry operated a toll-free hotline in Arabic, English, Hindi, Urdu, Tagalog, and other languages spoken by foreign residents through which workers were able to report delayed wage payments or other violations. MOHRE mobile van units also visited some labor camps to inform workers of their rights. The General Directorate of Residency and Foreign Affairs Dubai Office created the Taqdeer Award program, which rewards companies based on labor practices and grants them priority for government contracts.

The government-instituted revised standard contract for domestic workers aimed to protect domestic workers through a binding agreement between employers and domestic workers. The contract provides for transparency and legal protections concerning issues such as working hours, time-off, overtime, health care, and housing. Officials from some originating countries criticized the process, saying it prevented foreign embassies from reviewing and approving the labor contracts of their citizens. As a result some countries attempted to halt their citizens' travel to the UAE to assume domestic labor positions. Many still enter on visit visas, however, and then adjust status.

The government allowed foreign workers to switch jobs without a letter of permission from their employer. Labor regulations provide foreign employees the option to work without an employment contract or, in cases in which a contract was in force, to change employer sponsors after two years as well as within the first two years within the terms of the contract. The government designed this regulation to improve job mobility and reduce the vulnerability of foreign workers to abuse. The regulation, however, did not apply to agricultural or domestic workers.

One of the activities of the government-supported NGO, EHRA, was to promote the rights of workers. It conducted unannounced visits to labor camps and work sites to monitor conditions and reported violations to the MOHRE.

There were cases in which workers were injured or killed on job sites; however, authorities typically did not disclose details of workplace injuries and deaths, including the adequacy of safety measures. The MOHRE routinely conducted health and safety site visits. Dubai emirate required construction companies and industrial firms to appoint safety officers accredited by authorized entities to promote greater site safety.

Reports of migrant worker suicides or attempted suicides continued. In some cases observers linked the suicides to poor working and living conditions, low wages, and/or financial strain caused by heavy debts owed to originating-country labor recruitment agencies. The Dubai Foundation for Women and Children, a quasi-governmental organization, conducted vocational training programs with some elements aimed at decreasing suicidal behavior.